My Mother Is a Baker

My mother is a baker, a baker, a baker.
My mother is a baker.
She always goes like this, "Yum! Yum!"

My father is a driver, a driver, a driver.
My father is a driver. He always goes like this,

"Yum! Yum!
Vroom! Vroom!"

My sister is a singer, a singer, a singer.
My sister is a singer.
She always goes like this,

"Yum! Yum!
Vroom! Vroom!
La ta de da, and a toodly doo!"

5

My brother is a cowboy, a cowboy, a cowboy.
My brother is a cowboy. He always goes like this,

"Yum! Yum!
Vroom! Vroom!
La ta de da, and a toodly doo!
Yahoo!"

My doggie is a barker, a barker, a barker.
My doggie is a barker.
He always goes like this,

"Yum! Yum!
Vroom! Vroom!

La ta de da, and a toodly doo!
Yahoo!
Woof! Woof!"

My kitty is a snuggler, a snuggler, a snuggler.
My kitty is a snuggler.
She always goes like this,

"Yum! Yum!
Vroom! Vroom!
La ta de da, and a toodly doo!

Yahoo!
Woof! Woof!
Purr! Purr!"

My baby is a whiner, a whiner, a whiner.
My baby is a whiner. She always goes like this,
"Yum! Yum!
Vroom! Vroom!
La ta de da,
and a
toodly doo!

Yahoo!
Woof! Woof!
Purr! Purr!
WAH!"